Editor
Eric Migliaccio

Editor in Chief
Ina Massler Levin, M.A.

Creative Director
Karen J. Goldfluss, M.S. Ed.

Illustrator
Jessica Chrysler

Cover Artist
Barb Lorseyedi

Art Coordinator
Renée Mc Elwee

Imaging
Rosa C. See

Publisher
Mary D. Smith, M.S. Ed.

12/14

LEARNING TO

Cursive

GRADES 2-3

beetle

jellyfish

B b

J j

W w

whale

Practice writing:
- individual letters
- letter combinations
- words
- complete sentences

Teacher Created Resources

D1408750

Author

Susan Mackey Collins, M.Ed.

Teacher Created Resources
6421 Industry Way
Westminster, CA 92683
www.teachercreated.com
ISBN: 978-1-4206-2770-1

©2012 Teacher Created Resources
Reprinted, 2014
Made in U.S.A.

Teacher Created Resources

Table of Contents

Introduction

The activities in *Learning to Write Cursive* will help improve a student's ability to communicate through writing. Being able to write fluently in cursive is a skill all children need to learn. Cursive writing helps improve students' fine motor skills and allows them a new way to express themselves on paper. Most students are excited about learning a new style of writing and cannot wait to try cursive letter practice, such as the activities provided in *Learning to Write Cursive*.

Although much of the book is organized alphabetically, the pages in the book can be used in any order. One good way to start using the activities is to use the workbook pages that teach the letters in the child's name. All children enjoy seeing their own names written in cursive, and this will also help lend excitement to learning other letters and other words. Regardless of where you begin, both parents and teachers will find that children will enjoy the activities in *Learning to Write Cursive* while learning valuable skills.

Standards that are covered in *Learning to Write Cursive* include the following skills:

Uses grammatical and mechanical conventions in written compositions

- Writes in cursive

- Uses conventions of capitalization in written composition

- Uses conventions of punctuation in written compositions

- Uses conventions of spelling in written compositions (e.g., spells high frequency, commonly misspelled words from appropriate grade-level list; uses a dictionary and other resources to spell words; uses initial consonant substitution to spell related words; uses vowel combinations for correct spelling; uses contractions, compounds, roots, suffixes, prefixes, and syllable constructions to spell words)

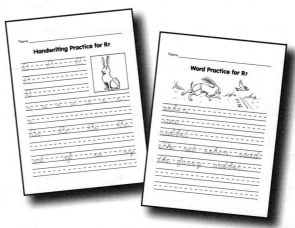

Handwriting Practice for Aa

a   a   a

a

a

a   a   a   a   a   a   a

a

Ab   Ac   Ad   Af

am   an   ap   ar   as

Word Practice for Aa

ant

acorn

anteater

The anteater ate an

acorn.

Handwriting Practice for Bb

B   B   B

B

B

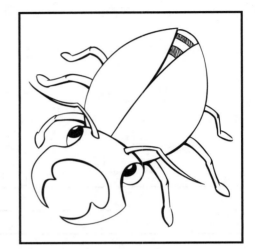

b   b   b   b   b   b   b

b

Ba   Be   Bl   Br

bb   bi   bo   bu

Word Practice for Bb

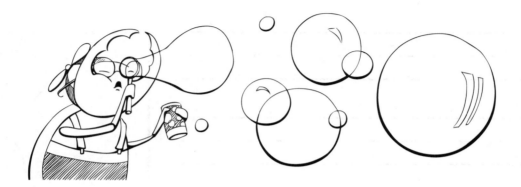

boy

beetle

bubbles

The boy beetle blew

bubbles.

Handwriting Practice for Cc

C — — C — — C

C

C

c — c — c — c — c — c — c

c

Ch — — Cl — — Cr — — Cu

ca — — ce — — ci — — co

Word Practice for Cc

cat

catch

canary

Can cats catch colorful

canaries?

9

Handwriting Practice for Dd

D   D   D

D

D

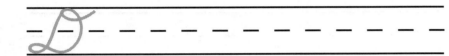

d

Da   De   Di   Do

dd   dl   da   dy

Word Practice for Dd

detective

dragon

dangerous

Detective Dino chased

the dangerous dragon.

Name _____

Handwriting Practice for Ee

E — E — E — E

E

E

e — e — e — e — e — e — e — e

e

Eg — El — Em — Es

ea — ed — ei — et

Word Practice for Ee

eagle

egg

eight

Eagle babies emerged

from all eight eggs.

Handwriting Practice for Ff

$\mathcal{F}$ — $\mathcal{F}$ — $\mathcal{F}$

$\mathcal{F}$

$\mathcal{F}$

f f f f f f f

f

$\mathcal{F}a$ — $\mathcal{F}e$ — $\mathcal{F}i$ — $\mathcal{F}o$

ff — fl — fr — fu

Word Practice for Ff

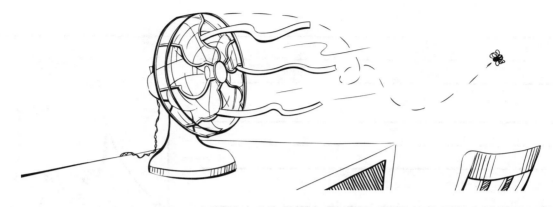

fly

flew

fan

That fly flew off of

Fred's fan.

Handwriting Practice for Gg

G G G

G

G

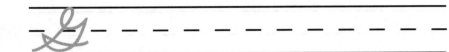

g g g g g g

g

Ga Ge Gi Gl

gh go gr gu

Word Practice for Gg

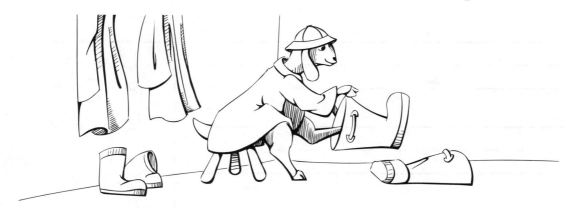

goat

green

galoshes

The goat wore huge

green galoshes.

Handwriting Practice for Hh

H   H   H

H

H

h   h   h   h   h   h   h

h

Ha   He   Hi   Ho

ha   he   hi   ht

Word Practice for Hh

hamster

has

habitat

The hamster has a

homey habitat.

Handwriting Practice for Ii

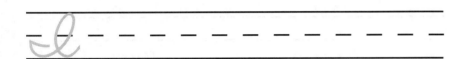

i i i i i i i

i

ic id ig im

if in is it

Word Practice for Ii

iguana

in

ivy

The iguana is in

Isaac's ivy.

Handwriting Practice for J j

Word Practice for J j

jellyfish

jiggling

joyfully

That jellyfish is

jiggling joyfully.

Handwriting Practice for Kk

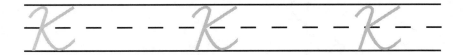

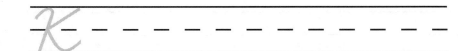

K

K

k k k k k k k

k

Ka Ke Ki Ko

ka ke ks ku

Word Practice for Kk

kangaroo

keep

key

The kangaroo is

keeping the key.

Handwriting Practice for Ll

$\mathcal{L}$ — $\mathcal{L}$ — $\mathcal{L}$

$\mathcal{L}$

$\mathcal{L}$

l — l — l — l — l — l — l

l

$\mathcal{L}a$ — $\mathcal{L}e$ — $\mathcal{L}i$ — $\mathcal{L}o$

la — ll — lo — lu

Word Practice for Ll

lion

leopard

lemonade

Leopards and lions

love lemonade.

Handwriting Practice for Mm

m — m — m

m

m

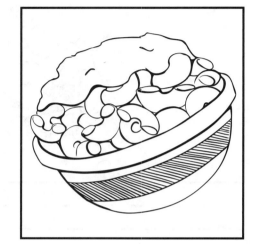

m — m — m — m — m — m — m

m

Ma — Me — Mi — Mo

ma — me — mn — mt

Word Practice for Mm

made

meal

macaroni

Mom made a meal of

ham and macaroni.

Handwriting Practice for Nn

n   n   n

n

n

n n n n n n n

n

Na   Ne   No   Nu

na   nn   no   nu

Word Practice for Nn

nurse

need

nap

The new nurse needed

a nap.

Handwriting Practice for Oo

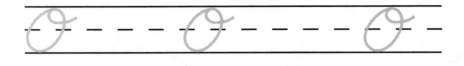

𝒪   𝒪   𝒪   𝒪   𝒪   𝒪   𝒪

𝒪

Ob   Of   Om   Os

oh   on   op   ow

Word Practice for Oo

ogre

onion

oatmeal

The ogre ate oatmeal

and onions.

Handwriting Practice for Pp

P   P   P

P

P

p   p   p   p   p   p   p

p

Pa   Pe   Po   Pu

ph   pi   pp   pt

Name _____

Word Practice for Pp

pass

pig

popcorn

Please pass the pig

the popcorn.

Handwriting Practice for Qq

Q   Q   Q

Q

Q

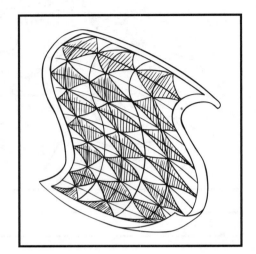

q   q   q   q   q   q   q

q

Qua   Que   Qui

qua   que   quo

Word Practice for Qq

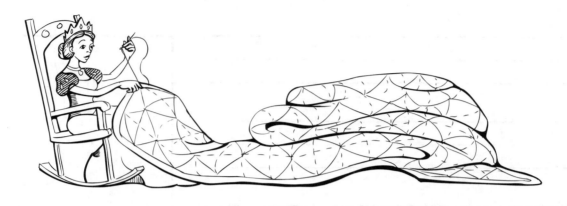

queen

quilt

quiet

The queen was quietly

quilting.

Handwriting Practice for Rr

R - - - R - - - R - - - R

R

R

r - - r - - r - - r - - r - - r - - r

r

Ra - - - Re - - - Ri - - - Ru

rd - - - rf - - - ro - - - ry

Word Practice for Rr

robin

race

rabbit

The red robin raced

the furry rabbit.

Name _____

Handwriting Practice for Ss

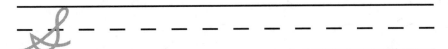

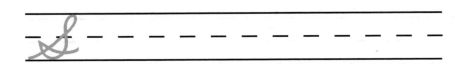

Word Practice for Ss

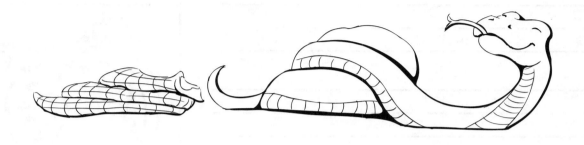

snake

shed

skin

The snake shed its

skin and sighed.

Handwriting Practice for Tt

$\mathcal{T}$ $\mathcal{T}$ $\mathcal{T}$

$\mathcal{T}$

$\mathcal{T}$

t t t t t t t

t

$\mathcal{T}a$ $\mathcal{T}h$ $\mathcal{T}i$ $\mathcal{T}u$

te to tr tw

Name _____

Word Practice for Tt

tiger

tangle

tail

The tiger's tail was

totally tangled.

Handwriting Practice for Uu

U   U   U

U

U

u   u   u   u   u   u   u

u

Uh   Un   Up   Us

ua   ug   um   ur

Word Practice for Uu

uncle

up

umbrella

The duck's uncle put

up his umbrella.

Handwriting Practice for Vv

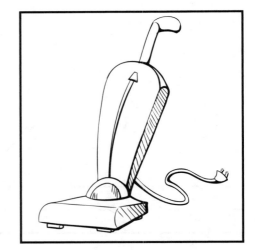

𝒱   𝒱   𝒱

𝒱

𝒱

𝓋 𝓋 𝓋 𝓋 𝓋 𝓋 𝓋

𝓋

𝒱a   𝒱e   𝒱i   𝒱o

𝓋a   𝓋e   𝓋o   𝓋y

Word Practice for Vv

very

vampire

vacuum

Very neat vampires

vacuum their caves.

Handwriting Practice for Ww

$\mathcal{W}$ --- $\mathcal{W}$ --- $\mathcal{W}$

$\mathcal{W}$

$\mathcal{W}$

w --- w --- w --- w --- w --- w --- w

w

$\mathcal{W}a$ --- $\mathcal{W}e$ --- $\mathcal{W}h$ --- $\mathcal{W}i$

we --- wo --- ws --- wy

Word Practice for Ww

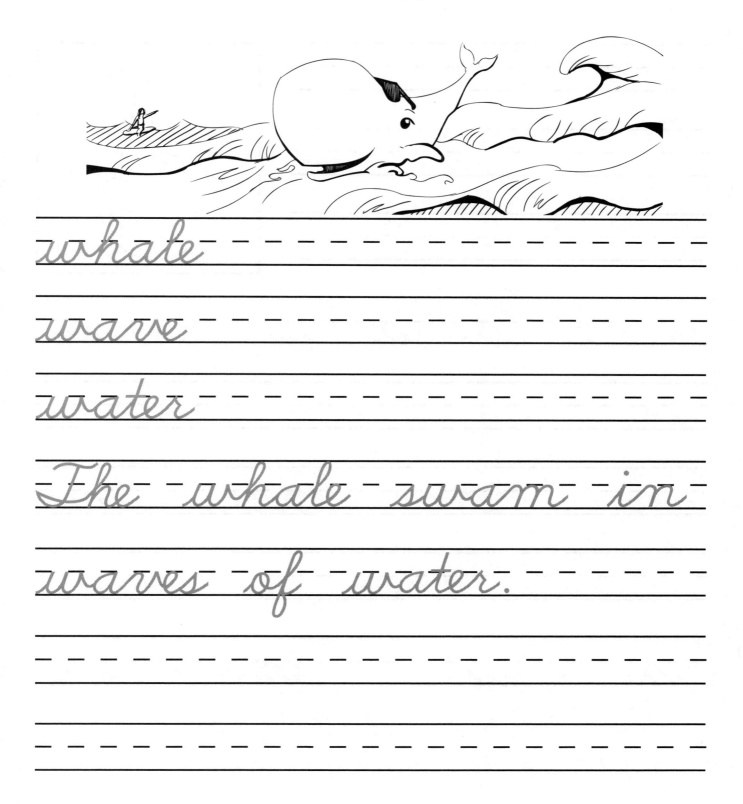

whale

wave

water

The whale swam in

waves of water.

Handwriting Practice for Xx

X   X   X

X

X

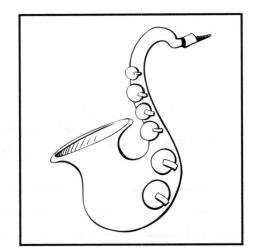

x   x   x   x   x   x   x

x

Xa   Xe   Xi   Xy

ax   ex   ix   ox

Word Practice for Xx

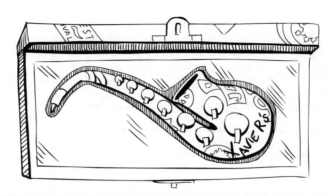

saxophone

extra

box

Xavier's extra sax is

in the box.

Handwriting Practice for Yy

Y   Y   Y

Y

Y

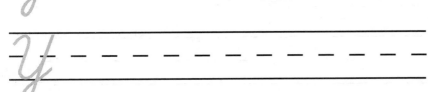

y   y   y   y   y   y   y

y

Ya   Ye   Yo   Ya

ya   yi   yo   ys

Word Practice for Yy

yak

yummy

yams

The yak always ate

yummy yams.

Handwriting Practice for Zz

Z   Z   Z

Z

Z

z   z   z   z   z   z   z   z

z

Za   Ze   Zi   Zo

ze   zl   zu   zz

Word Practice for Zz

zebra

zoo

zigzag

The zebra at the zoo

had zigzag strips.

Handwriting Affixes

An *affix* is a prefix or suffix that can be added to a root or base to form a new word. Words such as *unhappy* or *shyly* are examples of words with affixes.

un

pre

mis

ish

est

less

Words with Affixes

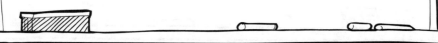

An *affix* is a prefix or suffix that can be added to a root or base to form a new word. Words such as *unhappy* or *shyly* are examples of words with affixes.

unhappy

prepay

greatest

selfless

Write a sentence in cursive that uses at least two of the words listed above.

_____

_____

_____

_____

Handwriting Homographs

Homographs are words that are spelled alike but have different meanings and pronunciations. Words such as *wound* and *minute* are examples of words that are homographs.

lives

bow

wind

tear

dove

read

Sentences with Homographs

He lives in that house.

Cats have nine lives.

The actress took a bow.

She wore a big bow
in her hair.

Handwriting Homophones

Homophones are words that are pronounced the same but are different in meaning and spelling. Words such as *eye* and *I* are examples of words that are homophones.

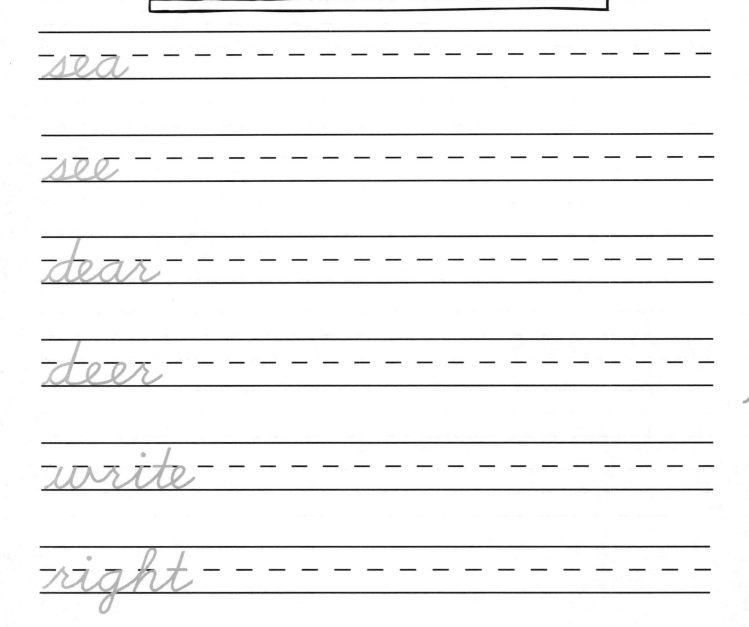

sea

see

dear

deer

write

right

Sentences with Homophones

I see a rainbow.

Fish swim in the sea.

Dee is my dear friend.

We saw a deer near the creek.

Name _____

Handwriting Lowercase Alphabet

a   b   c   d

e   f   g   h

i   j   k   l

m   n   o   p

q   r   s   t

u   v   w   x

y   z

Name _____

Handwriting Uppercase Alphabet

$\mathcal{A}$ - - - $\mathcal{B}$ - - - $\mathcal{C}$ - - - $\mathcal{D}$ - - -

$\mathcal{E}$ - - - $\mathcal{F}$ - - - $\mathcal{G}$ - - - $\mathcal{H}$ - - -

$\mathcal{I}$ - - - $\mathcal{J}$ - - - $\mathcal{K}$ - - - $\mathcal{L}$ - - -

$\mathcal{M}$ - - - $\mathcal{N}$ - - - $\mathcal{O}$ - - - $\mathcal{P}$ - - -

$\mathcal{Q}$ - - - $\mathcal{R}$ - - - $\mathcal{S}$ - - - $\mathcal{T}$ - - -

$\mathcal{U}$ - - - $\mathcal{V}$ - - - $\mathcal{W}$ - - - $\mathcal{X}$ - - -

$\mathcal{Y}$ - - - $\mathcal{Z}$ - - -

Handwriting Practice